pirates

SERIES EDITOR   DAVID SALARIYA
BOOK EDITOR   APRIL McCROSKIE

First American Edition 1996 by
Franklin Watts
A Division of Grolier Publishing
Sherman Turnpike
Danbury, CT 06816

©THE SALARIYA BOOK COMPANY LTD MCMXCVI
Library of Congress Cataloging-in-Publication Data
Steedman, Scott.
  Pirates / written by Scott Steedman : illustrated by
Nicholas Hewetson. – 1st American ed.
    p. cm. – (Worldwise)
  Includes index.
  Summary: Discusses the history and practices of pirates, covering such
aspects as weapons and flags, treasure and slaves, and pirate punishments.
  ISBN 0-531-14403-8 (lib. bdg.)   0-531-15297-9 (pbk.)
  1. Pirates – Juvenile literature.   I. Hewetson. N. J.   II. Title.
  III. Series.
G535.S74 1996   95-46730
910.4'5 – dc20   CIP AC

pirates

Written by
SCOTT STEEDMAN
Illustrated by
NICHOLAS HEWETSON

Series Created & Designed by
DAVID SALARIYA

FRANKLIN WATTS
A Division of Grolier Publishing
New York•London•Hong Kong
Sydney• Danbury, Connecticut

CONTENTS

So many stories have been told about pirates that it is often hard to know what to believe. Are they romantic heroes or bloody murderers of the seas? Pirates have been around for as long as ships and are still around today. But they were at their most popular in the Spanish Main (the Caribbean) from about 1500 to 1800.

Their daring and brutal exploits were the source of all the legends of buried treasure, desert islands, rum-running in the moonlight, and one-legged captains forcing their victims to walk the plank.

The Assyrians, Phoenicians, Greeks, and Romans were all troubled by pirates. They fought against them regularly.

In a Greek myth, the god Dionysus was captured by pirates. He became a tiger. The pirates leaped into the sea and turned into dolphins.

Roman and Greek ships on the Mediterranean Sea were terrorized by pirates. In the islands and inlets, sea robbers in fast galleys waited for slow trading vessels. Their prizes included slaves, wine, olive oil, wheat, silver, and gold. In the Dark Ages (A.D. 500-1000), Europe faced a new threat – the Vikings. In their longships, these pirates from the north raided far and wide, killing many people.

Roman slave market

The Romans ruled a slave empire. Anyone captured by pirates might end up for sale in a slave market like this one in Delos, Greece.

A pirate told Alexander the Great that he was just like him. "But since I raid in a small ship, I am called a pirate. You do it with a great fleet, so they call you emperor!"

Viking longships with flat bottoms could be rowed right up onto the beach.

The first attacks of the Viking Age (A.D. 800 – 1050) were on coastal villages. But soon Vikings were raiding as far inland as Paris, Russia, and even as far south as Baghdad.

9

NORTH AMERICA

SPANISH MAIN

SOUTH AMERICA

The Spanish Main was Spain's empire in the Americas. It stretched from Panama to the Orinoco River and included the Caribbean Sea.

Francis Drake was an English privateer who raided Spanish ships. After one voyage his ship almost sank, as it was so full of gold.

The Spanish viewed Drake as a brutal pirate. But Queen Elizabeth I of England knighted him in 1581.

Francis Drake

Privateers were private captains who were encouraged to attack enemy ships. In the 1500s, this was a cheap way for European countries to fight a war. In 1603, King James I of England banned privateering in the Caribbean.

Privateers in Hispaniola (present-day Haiti) formed gangs of lawless buccaneers. They were joined by escaped slaves and criminals. The buccaneers were ruthless pirates who terrorized the Spanish Main.

The Spanish plundered huge amounts of gold and silver from the New World and shipped it home in galleons or treasure ships.

Pieces of Eight were Spanish gold dollars. They were also called doubloons and were the main currency in the Spanish Main.

Henry Morgan

Buccaneers attacking a treasure ship in a fast, homemade outrigger with a triangular sail and a stolen cannon.

Henry Morgan, a Welshman, was a skilled buccaneer. He was knighted after capturing the rich Spanish town of Panama in 1671.

PIRATE FLAGS

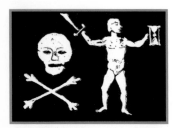

Captain Dulaïen

Jack Rackham

Christopher Condent

Hoist the Jolly Roger! A Spanish treasure ship has been sighted. Pirates preferred to rob treasure ships without a fight. They tried to scare the crew into surrendering by hoisting a terrifying flag. Every pirate had his own flag design – with skeletons, skulls, and swords – to strike fear into every sailor's heart.

All pirate crews included sailors who could repair damaged sails. They also used their needle and thread to sew flags to the captain's design.

Black jolly rogers with skulls were popular. They warned victims about the dangers of not surrendering.

Red flags were even more feared, because they meant that the pirates would kill any man or woman who dared to put up a fight.

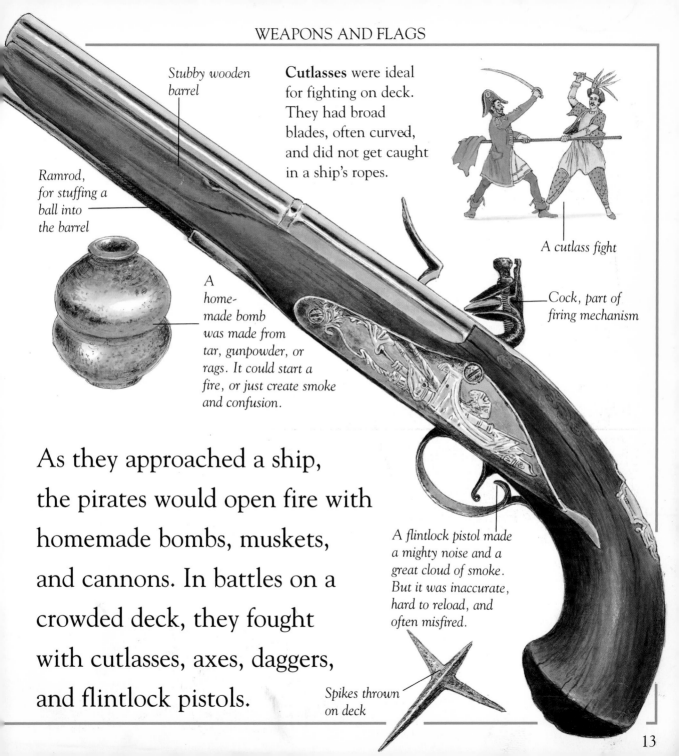

Stubby wooden barrel

Cutlasses were ideal for fighting on deck. They had broad blades, often curved, and did not get caught in a ship's ropes.

A cutlass fight

Ramrod, for stuffing a ball into the barrel

A home-made bomb was made from tar, gunpowder, or rags. It could start a fire, or just create smoke and confusion.

Cock, part of firing mechanism

As they approached a ship, the pirates would open fire with homemade bombs, muskets, and cannons. In battles on a crowded deck, they fought with cutlasses, axes, daggers, and flintlock pistols.

A flintlock pistol made a mighty noise and a great cloud of smoke. But it was inaccurate, hard to reload, and often misfired.

Spikes thrown on deck

Smoke and screams would

fill the air as a pirate ship drew alongside its

victim, a slow Spanish merchant ship.

Cannons and bombs exploded, and muskets

were fired. The raiders pulled the ship closer

with grappling hooks and slashed its ropes

to bring down the sails. Pirates were ready

to go aboard, yelling threats and waving

their weapons in the air. Turn the page to

see a trap laid by a clever pirate captain.

Full-blown battles were very rare. Pirates usually laid traps or used scare tactics. Captains knew that if they lost a fight, the pirates' revenge would be horrific. Most surrendered quietly.

A ship full of gold and

silver was every pirate's dream. Capturing one Spanish treasure ship could make the crew rich for life. But booty was rare. If the hold was empty, the pirates stole passengers' jewelry, watches, and weapons. They seized food, rum, ropes, cloth, maps, and even medicine. Then the pirates would share the booty. If they captured a slave ship, the pirates sold its human cargo.

Pirates divided the booty according to a strict code. The captain got the most. A man who had not fought got a part share, and a boy got half as much as a seaman.

Stories of buried treasure are mostly made up.

In pirate stories, "X" marks the spot where treasure is buried. In real life, it was the maps that were the real treasure. If pirates knew the area well, they could pounce on other ships and then disappear.

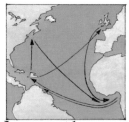

Atlantic slave trade triangle. Between 1500 and 1800, about 12 million slaves were shipped from Africa to the Americas.

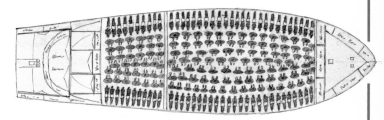

In one raid
Bartholomew Roberts (*see the next page*) captured 11 slave ships. He sold 10 back to their owners for a profit. One captain refused to pay, so his ship was set on fire, with 80 slaves on board.

For the voyage
across the Atlantic Ocean, the slaves were chained below decks with little food or water. Thousands died, but survivors were sold at public auction.

Slaves were often tied up and whipped.

Millions of African slaves were worked to death in appalling conditions on the plantations of the New World. No wonder many escaped slaves were happy to join pirate gangs!

"A Merry Life and a short one."

That was the motto of Black Bart (Bartholomew Roberts), probably the cleverest pirate ever to set sail. In four years he raided 400 ships, plundering off Africa, Brazil, and even Newfoundland. Blackbeard (Edward Teach) had crazy eyes and wild hair crackling with smoking gunners matches. He terrified even his own crew. Black Bart and Blackbeard had violent deaths.

Black Bart was a Welsh gentleman who liked fine clothes and drank tea. He was a good sailor and a brave fighter. He terrorized ships in the Caribbean and the Guinea Coast.

He was killed in a battle with an English warship in 1722. His crew of 254 included 70 African slaves and 18 French sailors, forced into piracy. Some 52 were hanged.

BLACK BART

Blackbeard's cruel ways and strange appearance made him into a legend. He was covered in pistols and daggers and shot his own crew on a whim.

Wild beard

Smoking match

Heavy musket

Edward Low was a cruel English pirate. He killed 53 Spanish captives with his cutlass, and he burned a French cook alive, saying he was "a greasy fellow who would fry well."

Low died in 1723 when his ship lost a battle with an English warship. Low was captured and hanged with 25 of his crew.

Blackbeard was killed off Ocracoke Island (North Carolina) on November 23, 1718, by Lieutenant Maynard of the English Navy.

Cutlass

BLACKBEARD

EDWARD LOW

21

Women pirates were

rare. At the time, women were not allowed on ships – they were considered bad luck. But pirates were rebels and a few rebellious women dressed up as men and joined them. The two greatest – Mary Read and Anne Bonny – were brave and daring.

Mary Read

Mary Read was a sailor and a soldier before she became a pirate. She was taken prisoner by "Calico Jack" Rackham and fought bravely beside his lover, Anne Bonny.

Anne Bonny left her husband to go pirateering with Rackham and Mary Read across the Caribbean. Their ship was captured in 1720. Rackham was hanged, but both women were spared because they were pregnant.

Anne Bonny

22

TURN THE PAGE TO SEE
INSIDE A PIRATE SHIP.

In China, female sailors were more common.

One great woman pirate, Madam Ching, had a fleet of 800 junks, 1000 smaller boats, and 80,000 pirates, both men and women.

When Calico Jack was hanged, Anne Bonny said, "Had you fought like a man, you need not have been hanged like a dog."

Madam Ching's fleet was broken up by wars with other pirates and the navy. She and her pirates surrendered and were officially pardoned.

Madam Ching in a fight

Being castaway was also called being marooned. One marooned pirate lived on berries, shellfish, and raw stingrays. But without fresh water, castaways had no hope.

Castaway on a desert island! This was the punishment pirates reserved for crew members caught stealing or trying to jump ship. Tropical islands were popular with pirates, because many were deserted and unmapped. One captain gave castaways *one bottle of powder, one bottle of water, one small firearm, and shot.* They were left to fish, hunt turtles, and pray that a passing ship would rescue them. The most famous castaway was Alexander Selkirk, the model for *Robinson Crusoe.*

The pirate ship sails away leaving a helpless castaway.

Selkirk was abandoned in 1704. For the next five years he lived on wild goats and palm cabbages, and made his own clothes and a house from goatskins.

Selkirk's island, Juan Fernandes, was off the coast of Chile. He was found by an English captain. The story inspired Daniel Defoe to write Robinson Crusoe.

Isle of Juan Fernandes.

Goat Quarters

Shade Bay

Royal Point

Open Bay

Wood Land

Sharpes Bay

Windy Bay

Fatt Anchoring

A rescued castaway

Hanged by the neck

until dead. This was the punishment for convicted pirates. After hanging, their bodies were sometimes dipped in tar and left to dangle by the waterside. The horrific sight was meant to discourage young sailors from going pirating. But very few pirates were ever brought to trial. Most died at sea, or lived to enjoy their booty.

Before hanging, a pirate was measured for a steel cage where his dead body would be displayed. The cage stopped relatives from cutting down the body and burying it.

The corpse was strung from a wooden frame called a gibbet.

Pirates could be brutal. But many stories are made up. No pirate ever made a victim "walk the plank." This punishment was invented by a story writer.

Barbary corsairs

Mediterranean Sea

North Africa

were Muslim privateers who attacked Christian ships in the Mediterranean. From about 1100 until 1830, the corsairs terrorized Europe from their bases on the south coast of the Mediterranean, known as the Barbary Coast. They dealt in slaves, selling them in African slave ports. It was a war against Christians, and the corsairs were heroes to other Muslims. Later, the term "corsairs" was also used for privateers from Malta and France.

Corsairs fought from galleys rowed by slaves. They rammed Christian ships, then leaped aboard and seized the crew.

Galleys had a ram and a cannon at the bow (front), and a single mast.

Unlike the Caribbean, the Mediterranean was well mapped and its waters were relatively calm.

Sir Francis Verney was an English sailor who joined the corsairs in 1608. He ended up as a slave on a Sicilian galley.

The corsairs were famous for their cruelty, and galley slaves were beaten mercilessly.

A typical galley had 20-30 wooden oars on either side. Each one was 6-10 feet (2-3 m) long and was rowed by as many as six men.

The "Barbarossa brothers," Aruj and Kheir-ed-Din, were famed for their red beards. Aruj died in 1518, but his brother fought the Spanish for 28 years more.

Réné Duguay-Trouin was a French corsair based in the port of St. Malo. In 23 years at sea, he captured over 300 vessels, including 16 English warships.

Other French corsairs fought far from home. Robert Surcouf attacked British ships from his base on Mauritius, in the Indian Ocean.

Captain Kidd was a pirate hunter who turned to plundering vessels in the Indian Ocean. He was hanged in 1701.

From 1690 to 1720, Madagascar was called Pirate Island. One visitor saw 1500 pirates there!

The East Indiamen ships were loaded in India, Hong Kong, and Indonesia.

High poop deck, where helmsman steered ship

Pirates were a real problem in the Indian Ocean in the 1600s and 1700s. They were chased out of the Caribbean and moved to the island of Madagascar. From here they raided Arab traders and Indian treasure ships.

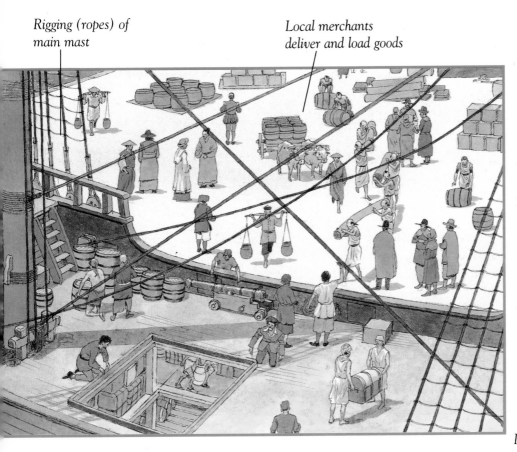

Rigging (ropes) of main mast

Local merchants deliver and load goods

Spices and silk were hard to sell in Madagascar. Many traders made their fortunes visiting pirate hideouts. Pirates would give them lots of money for these precious goods.

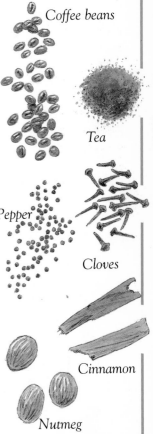

Coffee beans

Tea

Pepper

Cloves

Cinnamon

Nutmeg

But the pirate's favorite victims were East Indiamen. These were slow ships that carried gold and silver from Europe to Asia. They returned loaded with precious cargo like silks, spices, tea, and coffee.

Chinese pirates have raided

shipping in Asia for 1,500 years. The many islands and inlets of the coast are ideal hiding places for robber bands who break the law. In the 1600s, pirate fleets plundered European ships as they sailed to their new colonies in China and Southeast Asia. They were like private navies – the biggest fleets had hundreds of junks and thousands of bandits. The large pirate fleets were hunted down in the 1860s. But small-time pirates still attack ships in the China Sea.

Chinese pirates fought with spears, knives, swords, and blow pipes with poisoned arrows. They stole European guns when they could.

Chinese sailors, even pirates, worshipped T'ien Hou. This chubby goddess was said to calm storms and guard junks from misfortune.

Malaysia
SOUTH
CHINA
SEA
Indonesia

Bamboo batons stiffen sail

Square sails

Open deck

Thousands of local pirates controlled stretches of the China Sea. In the 1500s, Japanese fleets raided as far south as Malaysia.

This large junk was about 82 feet (25 m) long and 16 feet (5 m) wide. It was basically a trading junk with added cannon.

Poop (rear)

The captain lived with his wives and children in the poop (rear). This was the safest part of the ship. The crew lived on deck or in the hold with the ammunition.

English poet Lord Byron. His poem of 1814, The Corsair, glorified pirate life. It sold 10,000 copies in one day and inspired six operas.

Some of the best known pirates come from books, plays, and films – Captain Hook, Captain Blood, Long John Silver. After the real pirates died, people started telling stories about their cruel deeds. The most popular are still *Treasure Island*, by Robert Louis Stevenson, and *Peter Pan*, by J. M. Barrie. Hollywood adventure films have turned pirates into dashing heroes.

The first pirate novel was Robinson Crusoe by Daniel Defoe. He wrote it in 1719.

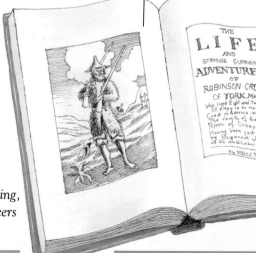

The best books on real pirates were written by people who sailed with them, such as George Roberts, and Alexander Exquemeling, who fought with buccaneers in the Caribbean.

BUCANIERS OF AMERICA: Or a True ACCOUNT OF THE Most Remarkable Assaults Committed of late Years upon the Coasts of The West-Indies By the BUCANIERS of Jamaica and Tortuga, Both ENGLISH and French.

THE LIFE AND STRANGE SUPRISING ADVENTURES OF ROBINSON CRUSOE OF YORK, Mariner

A cut-throat band helps Silver go for the treasure. They are defeated by Ben Gunn, a pirate they had marooned years before.

J.M. Barrie (right). His play Peter Pan was first performed in London in 1904. It tells the story of a boy's fight with evil Captain Hook.

Peter cuts off Hook's hand, so he wears an iron hook in its place.

Long John Silver is the evil one-legged pirate captain in Treasure Island (1883). He plots to seize the booty buried by another pirate, Captain Flint.

Stevenson was Scottish. He did not base Long John Silver on a real life pirate. Instead he was inspired by a friend, the dashing one-legged poet W.E. Henley!

Pirate from the comic operetta The Pirates of Penzance by Gilbert and Sullivan (1880).

USEFUL WORDS

Booty Goods stolen on a pirate raid.

Buccaneer Pirate, originally based in the Caribbean.

Corsairs Mediterranean privateers. Muslim corsairs sailed the Barbary coast and attacked Christian ships.

Cutlass Short sword, often with a curved blade.

Doubloon Another name for a Spanish gold dollar.

Gibbet Wooden frame for hanging a pirate's corpse.

Jolly Roger Pirate flag, usually red or black and decorated with skulls, crossbones, and swords. Each pirate had his own design.

Junk Chinese sailing ship, made of wood with a flat bottom and square sails.

Marooned To be left alone in an isolated place.

New World Name given to the Americas after colonization by Europeans in the 1500s.

Pieces of Eight Spanish gold dollars worth eight Spanish escudos each.

Pirate Robber or other criminal of the seas.

Plunder To steal goods.

Privateer Legalized pirates. They were issued with documents allowing them to attack enemy ships.

Spanish Main Spanish colonies in the Americas, stretching from Panama to the Orinoco River and including the Caribbean Sea.

INDEX

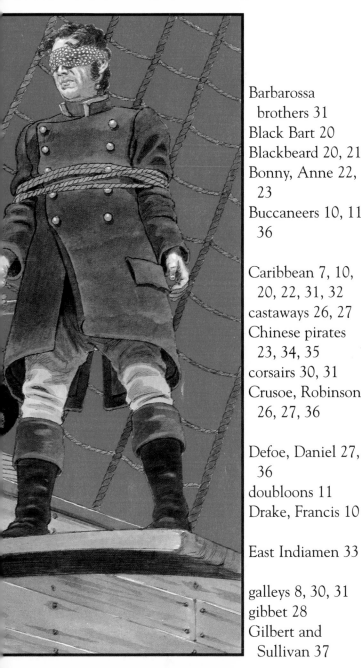

PRINTED IN BELGIUM BY

proost

INTERNATIONAL BOOK PRODUCTION